HOW TO PLAN YOUR NEW YEAR

Guide On How To Achieve Your Goals And Have A Successful Year

Table Of Contents:

INTRODUCTION:

Millions of people set New Year's Resolutions each year. Every year, individuals find themselves breaking those resolutions in some fashion within a few hours or days later. Many people will give up at this stage. They think—or persuade themselves—that they must be flawless. Once they commit even the smallest error, the resolution is null and void, and they are free to resume their previous behavior. They determine that their efforts to better their lives are ended for another year because they have fallen once more.

However, this way of thinking is wrong. Many of the greatest human ideas and achievements would never have been made if we all gave up at the first sight of challenges or temptations. **Consider Sir Edmund Hilary scaling Mount Everest or Michelangelo spending years in the most appalling conditions creating the Sistine Chapel ceiling.** The world today may be substantially different if they had given up at the first indication of hardship.

These two men, as well as countless others like them, shared the same quality: vision. They knew what they intended to accomplish, so they took the necessary actions to turn their vision into a reality.
Even though you probably won't ever want to do something as difficult as climbing Mount Everest, there are many challenges that we all desire to overcome that can feel just as high and nearly unattainable. But even if you've tried and failed at a goal in the past, envisioning the actions you need to take to complete it can frequently help you succeed. We'll talk about objectives in this manual that are realistic and doable for the majority of people. It is crucial to remember, though, that occasionally, even the most determined person in the world could experience material or physical

limitations that could prohibit them from fulfilling their deepest desires.

For instance, those who are born with disabilities might never be able to accomplish activities that we take for granted, like walking down the street or running, with both of their healthy feet firmly planted underneath them.

For another person who has been struggling his or her whole life with weight issues and the body image issues that can often accompany being overweight, the refrigerator and pantry might be their own personal Mount Everest.

Most of us have fairly common objectives that revolve around improving our lives in some way. If you have the correct attitude and determination, you may accomplish your objective of a new year, a new you through action. Even if you haven't met your objectives in the past, by understanding what has and hasn't worked in the past, you may position yourself for success this year rather than failure and create lasting changes.

Therefore, let's begin the next chapter by getting you started on making your unique resolutions for the new year and the new you.

CHAPTER ONE

MEANING OF RESOLUTION

Resolution is a word with more than one meaning. A resolution, on the other hand, refers to a commitment people make to improve themselves for the coming year. For the following year, the person resolves to put forth a significant effort.

A lot of people decide to try something new or make a change about themselves at the beginning of a new year. The resolution has been used in this way since the late 1700s. These older resolutions tended to be spiritual.

However, these days, New Year's resolutions are usually about living healthier, having more success, and finding greater satisfaction in life.

So, some common New Year's resolutions are to:

- Lose weight,
- Exercise more,

- Keep in contact with family and friends,
- Stop smoking,
- Save money,
- Go back to school,
- Cut back on alcohol,

or get more or better sleep.

One aspect of life may be all that some people resolve to get better at in the new year. Some people can feel that everything needs to be changed totally. These people might decide to start fresh in the new year!

Making a change and acting more responsibly is referred to as turning over a new leaf. You can start over at the beginning of the new year. This implies that you may easily wipe away all of your mistakes from the previous year, just like you would wash the chalk off a blackboard at school.

Just keep in mind that you should first learn from your failures before starting over. If not, you can find yourself starting over.

According to some lexicographers, the phrase originates from the board game Snakes and Ladders. You start on square one and move up the ladders to the final square to win this game. You might, however, be returned to the first square or the very beginning if you land on a snake.

Back to square one is a phrase that may have originated from the Hopscotch video game. This game similarly starts on a box with the number "1" written on it.

If your plans for the New Year are not working out at all, you may have to go back to the drawing board. This means that your plan or method is not working. So, you have to go back and develop a new solution to the problem. People who draw images, such as cartoonists, use a drawing board.

So, for many people, the New Year is a good time for a fresh start.

However, a lot of people don't keep their New Year's resolutions. They don't want to put themselves under further stress. Or they are content with their actions and the course of their lives.

Others might believe that there is no need to work so hard to alter yourself. They might concur that a leopard never changes its spots, as the proverb claims. This indicates that no amount of work will be able to change the way you were born. Change can be challenging, after all. It's challenging to get up early every day to exercise.

It's challenging to set aside time each day to study a new language or musical instrument. It may become much more challenging for people to alter their behavior as they age. You can't teach an old dog new tricks, as they say, perhaps.

IMPORTANCE OF RESOLUTION

Everyone can still stand to get better. Everyone adheres to the motto "New Year, New Me," yet they don't set resolutions. We set New Year's resolutions because we wish to improve upon who we already are. We set resolutions in order to push ourselves and live to the best of our abilities. As you can see, setting New Year's resolutions is vital.

I set goals for the new year because I wanted to challenge myself to become a better version of myself—not better than anyone else, but better than I was the day before. Becoming more responsible and doing all of my responsibilities when requested are my two personal resolutions. My two academic objectives are to continue being on the honor roll and to submit on time, for every subject, all of my assignments. As they say, "In with the new, out with the old," goals or resolutions are set to better oneself.

New Year's resolutions are significant because they provide people the chance to make positive changes in their life and set personal goals. It might be a good opportunity to think back on the previous year and pinpoint areas, like your work, relationships, and health, that require improvement. Setting objectives and creating a plan to reach them can boost accountability and motivation, resulting in a sense of success and satisfaction. It can also be a chance for people to stretch themselves and develop personally. To maximize the likelihood of success, it is crucial to maintain goals that are both reasonable and doable.

Everyone needs to push oneself because we all have tremendous potential; we just need the guts to see it. No one is flawless, and I believe we can all do things better. Setting goals will enable you to achieve your potential and live a better life. We can challenge ourselves with resolutions, but just ourselves, as we only aim to improve on yesterday's self. "If you want to live a happy life, connect it to a goal, not to people or things," as the proverb goes. Making resolutions or objectives will be a great benefit to us as we get ready for the future. Resolutions may seem silly to some, but there are several positive reasons to make them.

1. Resolutions Offer Opportunities for Change

Sometimes all we need is the chance to make a change in our life. That can be had in the New Year. For many, this might serve as the hard reset they require to make the changes they want because it marks the unmistakable end of one thing and the start of the next.

When we are working toward a goal, humans perform at their best. Our brains have evolved in this way. The cultural custom of making resolutions at the beginning of the year is the ideal time to establish this goal since having a vision for the future provides us motivation and encourages us to move forward. We should be completely prepared to take advantage of the society-approved way of goal setting that is literally built into our calendar: making resolutions.

2. Participation Provides Support

We have evolved to perform best in a group context, much as our brains have evolved to thrive on goal setting. Having a support system around them makes it simpler for many people to achieve their goals, and the New Year is no exception. I find solace in the idea that the majority of people are making resolutions at the same time as me when I make mine. Even though we may all be pursuing our own objectives, in a sense, we are all involved in this.

The way resolutions foster community is one of the reasons they have such a great heritage. It's nice to see everyone sharing their aspirations for the future and receiving encouragement in return.

3. Intention

The key to progress is being truthful with yourself about your situation right now and how far you are from your ideal state. Additionally, setting goals for your personal development and growth will help you succeed. Your fulfillment and happiness will both benefit from your intentionality. Your emotional and mental health benefit from your forward movement when you have a clear direction.

4. Hope And Engagement

Making New Year's resolutions is by nature cheerful and hopeful. You anticipate that things will improve for you, your professional situation, or your community. This optimistic outlook on the future in turn tends to spur action. You won't likely take action to better yourself or your community if you don't think tomorrow can be better. Consequently, being optimism has two advantages: it improves your mental health and motivates you to take action that benefits people around you.

5. Responsibility

Most New Year's resolutions affect other people in some way. Even when they are focused on improving oneself, they also have an impact on communities, families, and friends. Your goal to improve your health will help you live longer for your loved ones and friends. Your decision to avoid putting things off will help your coworkers and you function as a cohesive team. Additionally, your plans to volunteer at the community garden more often will contribute to the local food supply. Making commitments for the new year is a great approach to put your attention on yourself while also thinking about your larger responsibility—and to increase and multiply your positive effects on others.

6. Inspiration

You tend to inspire others when you strive to improve yourself, what you do, or how much you provide. People learn most effectively by observing how others behave. People continuously pick up on other people's choices and cues, even if they're not consciously aware of it. Putting your attention on the future and on growth inevitably motivates others around you.

Resolutions provide practice setting goals: Setting goals is an essential part of life. Goals are important because they give your life a broad direction. According to the self-improvement book, a goal is a map that may show you where you are going and the route you need to follow to get there. Success\sConsciousness. Resolutions can be enjoyable, non-binding objectives. Consider them as practice runs for more significant life adjustments.

7.   Resolutions   Offer   Time   For Reflection:

People rush through daily life far too frequently without pausing or slowing down to properly consider the effects of their choices. According to the wellness site, resolutions help you focus on the past, present, and future to determine what has been working and what might need to be modified to provide a boost.

It could act as a catalyst for progress. Resolutions can act as the trigger that ultimately rights the ship when something in your routine, personal health, or relationships isn't functioning.

8. Resolutions Can Promote Self-esteem And Empowerment

Making and keeping resolutions can give you the sense of accomplishment that comes from setting goals and seeing them through. Making a five-pound weight loss goal and then seeing the results on a scale can be a great motivator to change for the better. Small goal accomplishments can also increase self-esteem.

It is frequently created at the start of a new year. These initiatives may give people the inspiration and guidance they require to transform their lives for the better.

9. Resolutions Can Provide A Fresh Start

New Year, new YOU! It's almost like pressing the "reset" button to start the new year by making a New Year's resolution. You get to choose how to approach your goals and set new ones or review previous ones. More meditation you want? recommit to journaling? more time with family and friends? Whatever they are, New Year's resolutions provide you the chance to think back and refocus.

11. Resolutions Can Provide Clarity For Goals

You get direction by setting goals in writing. They enable you to chart your future course. Without goals, you waste your time, resources, and efforts, which makes you feel overburdened and unprepared for potential chances.

12. Resolutions Can Make Us Feel Good

Have you ever achieved something that first seemed impossible? When you make a promise to yourself and keep it, it feels like that. The same holds true for resolutions. Making a commitment to better yourself and achieving those goals gives you the motivation to keep going. Whatever it may be, nothing feels better than demonstrating to yourself that you are capable of doing anything you set your mind to.

Ultimately, humans are at their best when they have a goal to reach, and what better way to hit the reset button on your goals than with a few New Year's resolutions?

TIPS FOR MAKING RESOLUTIONS
TO BE SUCCESSFUL

This year, do you plan to reinvent yourself? Or at the very least use the start of the year as a long overdue justification to break old habits or adopt new ones?

Yes, it's time to review how to keep a new year's resolution once more. It's that time of year when we feel like we need to make a fresh start and turn over a new leaf. This is the period when we erroneously believe that the start of a new year will miraculously bring the impetus, drive, and perseverance we need to change ourselves.

New Year's Day is customarily thought of as the perfect occasion to begin a new phase of your life and the day on which you must make your crucial new year's resolution.

Being in the middle of the holiday party and vacation season, the beginning of the year is unfortunately one of the worst periods to make significant changes to your routines.

This is the reason that more than 80% of New Year's resolutions fail.

Don't set yourself up for failure this year by vowing to make huge changes that will be hard to keep. Instead, follow these seven steps for successfully making a new year's resolution you can stick to for the long term.

Here are a few tricks for setting and keeping your goals this year.

1. Pick One Thing

Don't attempt to alter every aspect of your life or way of living at once if you want to make changes. It will fail. Choose one aspect of your life to start changing instead.

Making a precise resolution that you can measure against will help you realize exactly what change you're aiming to accomplish.

After a month or so, if the first adjustment is a success, you can move on to the next one. You still have the option to be a whole new you at the end of the year by making modest adjustments one at a time, and this is a far more practical approach.

To put this into perspective, 50% of people plan to get fitter in the new year. Don't choose a New Year's resolution that you know will fail, such as running a marathon if you weigh 40 pounds too much and have trouble breathing when climbing stairs.

If that's the case, decide to set goals for the new year that will inspire you to go for daily walks. Perhaps this will help you lose weight.

Once you've mastered that habit, you can advance to running in short bursts, continuous running by March or April, and a marathon after the year. Which habit do you wish to modify the most?

2. Plan Ahead

Making resolutions for the new year is no easy task. It's even tougher to learn how to keep resolutions.

Do not wait until the last minute if you want to succeed. To ensure you have the resources you need when you need them, you should investigate the change you're making and make a strategy.

Here are a few things you should do to prepare and get all the systems in place and ready to make your change.

Read up on it – Go to the library and get books on the subject. Whether it's quitting smoking, taking up running or yoga, or becoming vegan there are books to help you prepare for it. Or use the Internet.

Plan for success – Prepare everything in advance to ensure success. If you decide to start running, be sure to have your sneakers, outfit, hat, sunglasses, and iPod ready with some upbeat music.

You could even find a partner to work with. Working alongside a buddy or coworker can help you make better decisions because, according to study, self-control can be contagious.

There are no valid defenses. One of the reasons resolves fail is due to this.

3. Anticipate Problems

Your aim will not be simple to achieve. Make a list of the issues that will arise since there will be issues. If you give it some thought, you'll be able to foresee issues during particular times of the day, with particular individuals, or in particular circumstances.

Work out strategies to deal with them when they inevitably arise once you've identified the periods that will likely be difficult. You can learn how to keep new year's resolutions if you keep this advice in mind.

4. Pick A Start Date

These adjustments don't have to be made on January 1st. That's a pearl of common wisdom, but if you're sincere about making changes, choose a day when you'll be rested, fired up, and surrounded by inspiring individuals. I'll hold off till my kids' February start of the new school year.

Choosing a date doesn't always work out. Wait until your entire body and mind are prepared to take on the challenge. When the ideal moment arrives, you'll know when it is.

Setting a schedule for achieving your goals is advised, just like choosing a start date.

By setting smaller goals along the road, you may give yourself plenty of time to complete your New Year's resolution. Your progress will be easier to see if you can mark off these minor accomplishments.

For instance, you might schedule "vegan days" twice a week throughout January and February if you wanted to eat healthily. As the months pass, you can progressively raise it.

5. Make Them Relevant

Most resolutions fail because they are built on a quality about yourself that society tells you needs to alter. The resolution to lose weight is the best illustration of this because it is one of the most popular and also one of the most likely to fail. Why? This objective is not only vague but is also predicated on outside evaluation. You shouldn't make resolutions for other people. They ought to work for you.

Your resolution should be founded on a value that you strongly believe in and should be something that you are enthusiastic about. I want to spend less time at work and more time with my family. This is based on a value, whereas "I want to lose weight" is a resolution based on a social expectation. Finding a resolution that ignites your passion increases the likelihood that you'll stick with it and succeed.

6. Track Your Progress

Nothing inspires you more than realizing how far you've come. Tracking your progress will help you feel more confident that you are moving on the correct path. This is now simple to achieve because of technology.

For instance, you could use an app to mark the days that you made progress toward your objective. You can also develop a spreadsheet that will help you visualize your progress if you want to go the extra mile.

You'll be more driven to continue on the right path once you see how far you've come and how well all of your sacrifices paid off. For days when you feel like your motivation is waning, reviewing all the effort you have put in is a great tactic.

7. Remember Your Past Failures

Take a look at your past failures as one of the best resolution-making tips you will ever discover. You won't make those errors again if you do it this way.

Your self-esteem will suffer greatly if you keep making the same errors year after year.

Consider your prior lapses if you want to make new year's resolutions that you won't keep. What decisions did you make that allowed you to escape it? Did anything inspire you to put forth more effort toward accomplishing your goal?

Be as adaptable as you possibly can. There is nothing wrong with changing your goal to something more achievable. Who knows, if you switch up your strategy, you might have better outcomes.

8. Take Small Steps

Change takes time to manifest. Many people become discouraged and give up on their resolutions when they don't materialize as quickly as they anticipated. This can be greatly helped by creating a plan with tiny, doable tasks, which also makes it simpler to carry them out. Your aim does not have to be a single, overarching objective; it can instead be broken down into several smaller objectives.

It can also be beneficial to admit that you're not in a rush to achieve your goal. This keeps you from ever feeling behind and gives you an excuse to give up on your resolve. Give yourself some space; you can handle things when the time is right.

It may feel impossible to follow through on your resolution, but it doesn't have to be. When it comes to resolutions, the journey is just as important as the final goal.

With our resolutions, we are developing new routines and ways of living while also discovering a little bit more about ourselves. Take your time since the journey is what matters most.

9. Make Them Manageable

Our New Year's resolutions receive a lot of attention, possibly more than is required. Because resolutions are so important, many people set goals that are a little out of their league, which can leave them feeling defeated and jaded when they aren't achieved.

Get precise about your resolutions rather than making general ones such, as "I want to lose weight," "I want to stop eating out," or "I'm going to start going to the gym." Make your resolution more specific so that you can actually carry it out, and then proceed from there.

It's possible to transform "I want to start going to the gym" into "I want to make it to the gym at least once a week." Once you've done that, you can always change your resolution to something like, "I want to work out at least twice a week." This not only makes it simple for you to set goals, but it also gives you a wonderful tool to monitor your progress. You'll have visited the gym at least twelve times by the conclusion of the third month!

10. Go for It

Go all out on your big day. Commit and record it on a card when learning how to make a new year's resolution.

All you need is a single, compact phrase that you can keep in your wallet. Keep it near your bed, in your car, and on your bathroom mirror for an additional boost in motivation. Your commitment card will say something like this:

- **I enjoy a clean, smoke-free life.**
- **I stay calm and in control even under times of stress.**
- **I'm committed to learning how to run my own business.**
- **I meditate daily.**

11. Accept Failure

Failure is common, regardless of how big or little your ambitions are. Don't despise yourself if you do falter and sneak a smoke, skip a walk, or yell at the kids one morning.
It's okay to make mistakes occasionally. Take note of the factors and bad behaviors that contributed to this setback and commit to learning from them.

Reduce your alcohol intake if you are aware that it causes you to crave cigarettes and to sleep the next day. Get up earlier or prepare things the night before if you know that the morning rush before school makes you yell.
The secret to success is perseverance. You will succeed if you set goals, keep trying, and keep trying.

12. Plan Your Rewards

Make sure to master this phase in making new year's resolutions because small prizes can be a terrific motivational boost during the toughest initial days.

After that, you can probably treat yourself once a week to anything that makes you happy, whether it's a magazine, a long-distance call to your encouraging friends and family, a nap, a trip to the movies, or something else. You can choose an anniversary reward at the end of the year after changing the rewards to monthly in the future. Something you'll eagerly anticipate. You will have earned it and you deserve it.

Whatever your plans and set goals are for this year, I'd do wish you luck with them but remember, it's your life and you make your luck.

Decide what you want to do this year, plan how to get it, and go for it

CHAPTER TWO

HOW TO PLAN YOUR NEW YEAR

New year, new you. You don't have to wait until the first day of the new year to make resolutions. Anytime is a fantastic opportunity to make plans for your year that will help you achieve your goals, both for yourself and others. It could seem like a daunting task, but by determining what you need to accomplish and how to achieve it, you can use several tools and techniques to realize your aspirations.

Everybody wants to have a better life in the next new year. Nobody wants to spend their entire life living the same year 75 times over. We don't want that, though. We are wired for growth, accomplishment, and success as humans.
And for this reason, it's crucial to develop your year-ahead planning skills. One of the most crucial elements to success and leading a better life is planning. But the majority of

individuals have no notion of how to organize their year or their lives.

And in this guide, I will share with you simple steps you can follow to plan your year so that you can set yourself up to win in life.

You see, success is about winning your day. When you win your day, you will win your week. When you win your week, you will win your month. And when you win your month, guess what, you will win your year.

And of course, if you continue to win and score every year, you will win your life. That's how success is created. Below are the steps to help you plan your year so that you can win in the game of life...

1. Reflect On The Past Year:

Consider the past year in terms of your accomplishments, things you would have done differently, and lessons you took away from it.

Establish definite, detailed goals for each aspect of your life that you would like to improve. Make sure your objectives are time-bound, meaningful, quantifiable, and realistic.

2. Create A Plan Of Action:

Divide your objectives into manageable, smaller steps. Create an action plan that specifies how you will accomplish each target and the resources you will require.
Additionally, analyze potential hindrances and difficulties and devise solutions.

3. Prioritize Your Goals:

Determine which objectives are most essential to you and order them in that order.
Whether it's a journal, accountability partner, or setting reminders, find a means to hold yourself responsible for reaching your goals.

Keep track of your development frequently and adjust as necessary. As you advance through the year, keep in mind that development may not always be linear and that it is acceptable to review, reevaluate, and make adjustments.

Always keep in mind that defining and accomplishing goals is a continual process. It's crucial to monitor your progress and change as necessary. Don't be too hard on yourself if you didn't accomplish all of your resolutions; making new year's resolutions is a process, not a one-time thing. Be kind to yourself.

4. Envision the Ideal Year In Your Head

Envision the ideal year you want. How do you want your future to look like? Do you want to...

- To reduce weight and regain your fitness?

- Eliminate all of your debt and take charge of your life?
- More money saved for investments or purchasing a new home?
- Get married and establish a family of your own?
- Stop smoking, it's bad for you.
- Produce and release a book?
- Start a side hustle online business?

If you are willing to imagine, plan, and take significant effort, you can achieve anything.

So, whenever you're planning your year, start by imagining what you want it to look like.

And don't forget to add as much intrigue as you can. Why? You won't ever look forward to realizing your dreams if they are not thrilling. And you won't ever want to act if you're not motivated to realize your dreams.

5. Create A Vision Board

You should build a vision board for your goals for the year to help you plan them more effectively and to keep them intriguing. Constructing what you desire much more concretely by making a vision board can be a great tool in assisting you in making your dream year a reality.

You give your aspirations and goals a place and time to live in your life when you make a vision board. To enable your mind to realize the visions in your head, you translate them into actual visuals and pictures. Finding images that reflect what you desire and gluing them to a board so that you can see them and envision them every day is all that is required. Your vision boards will serve as a trigger for your dreams and goals, reminding you to act every day.

6. Create An Actionable Plan

It is time to develop an actionable strategy for your 90-day goals after you have determined what they are.

Because they stop at the "goal-setting" level, this is where the majority of people fall short. They plan nothing, but they do set goals.

To ensure that your mind is fully aware of the steps you must take to reach your goals, you must plan them out and develop an executable strategy.

How should you make your plans? I employed a three-column layout. Take a piece of paper and divide it into three columns by drawing two lines across it.

- You can include your initiatives and goals in the first column.
- Your approach and plans should go in the second column.
- The third column is for actions and things you should do.

You can plan your objectives and tasks using this method throughout the year. Your annual planning doesn't have to be difficult, but you must make sure that your objectives are precise and that your action plans are understandable.

Your mind won't know what to do when your action steps are vague; as a result, it will either do nothing or put off taking action. Stop allowing that to happen to you. To enable you to take action, make sure your actionable steps are precise and unambiguous.

7. Turn The Actions Into Habits

If you want to accomplish your goals, motivation is not enough by itself. Creating a plan for your year in advance is just the beginning. The most crucial step is to start acting and moving forward.

No matter how good your strategy is, if you don't put it into action, it will fail.

You should develop habits by repeating actions and behaviors. You want to develop this behavior into a habit, for example, if your objective is to lose weight and you should exercise for at least 30 minutes each day. When a behavior is ingrained in you, you will carry it out without thinking about it whenever the occasion arises.

Because of this, you need to create positive habits that will help you keep to your objectives and plans. Most people only act and work toward their objectives when they are motivated. However, when they lack drive, they will just put off doing something and do something else in its place.

And this is the primary distinction between those who are successful and those who are not. Whether or not they are motivated, successful people decide to act. Even when they don't feel like it, they continue to work. And for that reason, they are prosperous.

You must behave similarly. Building solid habits are the only method to ensure that you act and carry out your objectives and goals.

8. Review Your Progress Weekly

When did you last evaluate your progress? The majority of individuals don't, which is why most of them don't succeed.

You must continuously assess your progress to make sure you are moving toward your objectives and realizing your ideal year.

I advise you to at the very least evaluate your plans, goals, and development once per week. You should perform it at least once every week, albeit not necessarily daily.

Just remind yourself of your intentions and ambitions. then take heed of what you did incorrectly the prior week. After that, you should improve your plan for the following week. By doing this, you can ensure that you are constantly progressing and moving in the proper direction. You see, weighing oneself is the first thing you must do if you want to lose weight. You weigh yourself while standing on the scale.

Unfortunately, most people don't track their progress when setting and attaining goals.

They believed that defining goals was a one-time task. They believe that all they need to do is make one plan, and everything will just come by itself. No, things don't operate in a way. Every day, or at the very least once each week, you should examine and revise your goals.

You re-engage with what you want to accomplish in your life when you examine your goals and make a fresh plan. And this will encourage you to be proactive and take action.

9.Celebrate Your Progress

The next step is to recognize your accomplishments, not simply victories. You should rejoice as long as you are going forward and doing the action.

And by celebrating, I don't just mean throwing a late-night bash. When you do a tiny activity, like writing an article, you can pat yourself on the back and consider it a small victory.

You don't have to wait till you accomplish the major objective before you can rejoice. You will have to rejoice more as you increase your celebrations. Making progress makes you feel good, which trains your brain to work harder and accomplish more. Most people hold off until they succeed to feel good. They make statements like...

- When I am debt-free, I will be joyful.
- When I get rid of the excess weight, I'll feel great.
- When I become a best-selling author, I will be very happy.

No, you don't have to put off finding fulfillment and happiness. Feel happy now and gladly achieve rather than waiting to feel good after you accomplish something.

10. Time Block To Make Sure You Act

Time blocking is one of the most effective methods for preparing your year in advance. This method will guarantee that the work gets done. What you must do is straightforward. Once you've organized your day and know what actions you need to take, all that's left to do is set aside time to ensure that the action takes place.

Here is one instance. You can set aside two hours today if you need to compose an article. You can reserve the hours of 10 AM to 12 PM completely for article authoring.
You won't do anything else during these two hours than write the post. This will allow you to work on your task with complete concentration and no outside distractions.
If someone wants your attention, you will have to decline their request and inform them that you are not available at this moment and that you will contact them again later.
Time blocking functions as follows.
Imagine setting aside an hour or two each day to work toward your objectives. You will have taken so many steps and made so

much progress toward your goals in a year. You will achieve your goals.

11. Review Your Year

Reviewing your year should be the final action you take. Yes, you begin your year by planning, and you finish it by doing a review.

As you already know, it's critical to reflect on your actions to learn from both the good and the bad so that you can improve your life. Your annual review doesn't have to be difficult.

To review your year, just ask yourself these 3 questions:

- What transgressions did I commit during the past year?
- What actions did I take correctly during the past year?
- What are some things I can do better or more in the upcoming year?

Here is another method for reviewing the past year. Just make a list of three to five activities you'll start, stop, and do:

- What are the three things I'm going to start doing this year?
- What three things will I no longer do in the upcoming year?
- What are the three things I'll keep doing in the upcoming year?

Although it's labeled "review your year," it's better when done once every three months. Why? Because you can assess what is working and whether you are on the correct route now rather than having to wait a year. Every three months, you can assess and analyze to make sure you are moving on the right path.

IN CONCLUSION:

Make an effort to join the small percentage of people who stick to their New Year's resolutions. However, be aware that even if you don't keep everyone, the process of making objectives and working toward them can benefit both you and other people.
Everyone has experienced difficulty making and keeping new year's resolutions. Therefore, do not be too hard on yourself if you have a history of breaking your resolutions. Hope is still present. Long-term dedication is what distinguishes success from failure.

It takes talent to organize your year in advance. Additionally, there is only one method to do it—whatever works best for you. Planning more will make you better at it. And the more effective you are at planning, the more probable it is that you will accomplish your objectives and realize your aspirations.

Nobody ever made a plan to be poor, obese, sluggish, or foolish. When you don't have a plan, those things are what will take place. So, go to work on your annual plan straight away.